Song for the Whooping Crane

Written by
Eileen Spinelli

Illustrated by
Elsa Warnick

EERDMANS BOOKS FOR YOUNG READERS

GRAND RAPIDS, MICHIGAN   CAMBRIDGE, U.K.

To Susan Cherner, who taught me that women can fly
and to Ellyn, Phyllis, and Jean, who fly with me still.
—E. S.

To Linda Zuckerman.
For all you are, thank you.
—E. W.

With special thanks to the International Crane Foundation in
Baraboo, Wisconsin, for their invaluable research assistance.

Text copyright ©2000 by Eileen Spinelli
Illustrations copyright ©2000 by Elsa Warnick
Published 2000 by Eerdmans Books for Young Readers
An imprint of Wm. B. Eerdmans Publishing Company
255 Jefferson Ave S.E., Grand Rapids, Michigan 49503
P.O. Box 163, Cambridge CB3 9PU U.K.
Printed in Hong Kong
00 01 02 03 04 05   7 6 5 4 3 2 1

Library of Congress Cataloging-in-Publication Data
Spinelli, Eileen
Song for the whooping crane / written by Eileen Spinelli; illustrated by Elsa Warnick.
p. cm.
Summary: A poetic celebration of the whooping crane,
one of the rarest birds in North America.
ISBN 0-8028-5172-X (alk. Paper)
1. Whooping crane - Juvenile poetry. 2. Children's poetry, American.
[1. Whooping crane - Poetry. 2. Cranes (Birds) - Poetry. 3. American poetry.]
I. Warnick, Elsa ill. II. Title.

PS3569.P5457 S6 2000
811'.54 — dc21   00-022937

nce whooping cranes nested on prairies
in numbers you would be all day counting.
Now they are one of the rarest birds in
North America . . .

In the far North
when October spills
across the ice
and the wind sweeps high

the wild whooping cranes fly.

They fly south over cities,
over silvery plains,
through spattering sleet
and wintery rains.

Upon this brave journey
the frosty moonrise gleams.
Come see!
Step out from dappled doorways,
leave your dreams.

At last
the cranes' long faithful flight
is done.

Below,
the ponds and marshes
sparkle in the sun.

Some cranes spiral from the clouds,
and some cranes skim,
and one crane — look! —
reckless with delight
dives downward on a whim.

By day they search for fish and snails.

Some even have a playful flair
for chasing dragonflies about
or tossing wild berries in the air.

They trumpet startling calls
that fall on ears
for miles around —
"Ker-loo, ker-lee-oo!"

By night,
when stones reflect
the scattered stars
and dark falls deep,
the whooping cranes
wade into shallow pools
and go to sleep.

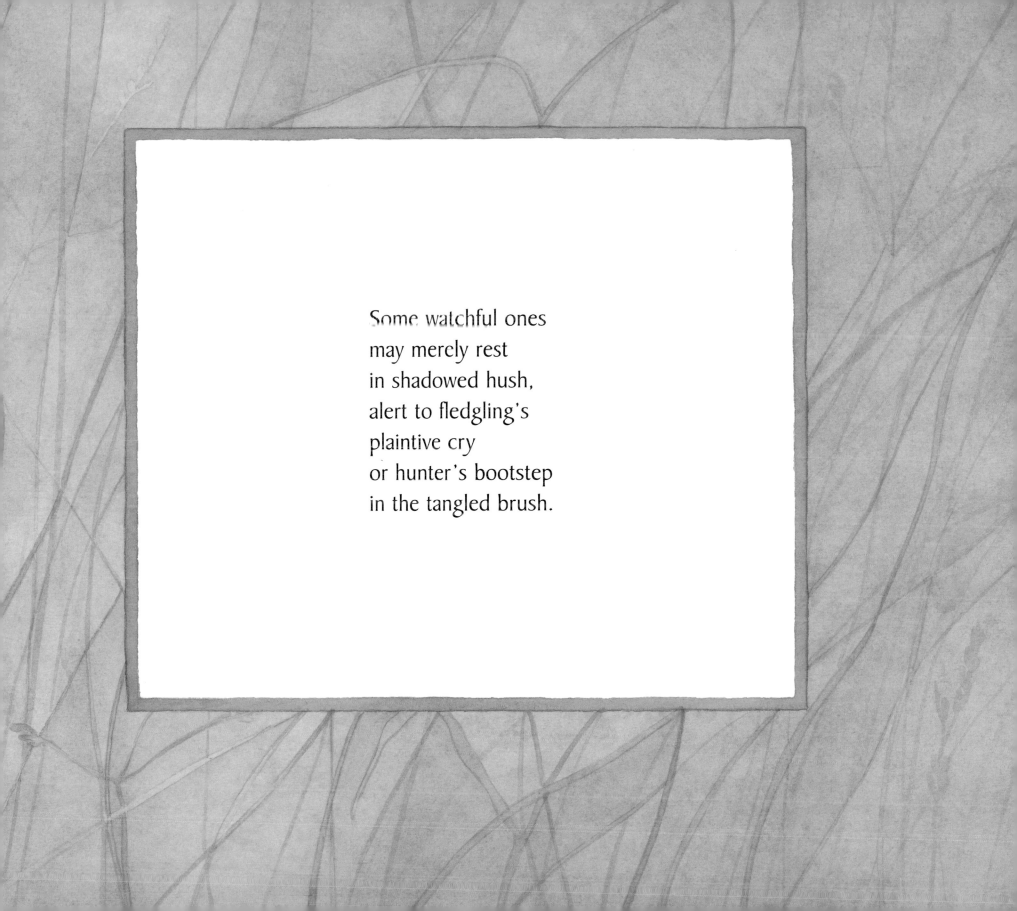

Some watchful ones
may merely rest
in shadowed hush,
alert to fledgling's
plaintive cry
or hunter's bootstep
in the tangled brush.

And now —
the sweetest thing of all —
they dance!

They bow,
they leap,
they flap their wings,
they prance
in pairs,
or one by one,
or as a flock entire —
bobbing . . . bobbing . . .
graceful
heads up higher,
higher.

And then when
blossom-scented April nears
the whooping cranes take off
like feathered spears.
Once more to northern nesting grounds
they go.

May it always be so.